GIFTS IN THE KEY OF NATURE

Philip J. Taylor

Arum Press
Montreal

Second Edition

Recalling times lived in South Africa and Canada and moments
in those times and remarkable people I'd met, I speak of their
extraordinary and everyday triumphs and challenges which touched my
senses. Joys of Freedom are celebrated in the spirit of Nature's green and
riotous garden party. Frolic unbridled resonates with a motif of rhythmic
leaps and bounds and sheer fun. Keeping Faith only serves to sober one
in abiding beliefs to stay alive and stay the course.
Marking the end as a new beginning, Watercress Epilogue takes
this collection out on a whimsical note fragrant with the aroma of orange
blossoms.

Acknowledgments

I would like to thank my parents Hester and Benjamin Taylor for their gifts of life. Their nourishing sacrifice and indelible example are written into my soul. The music of my sisters' and brother Rhoda, Eleanor, and Norman. We still hear Peter, Linda, and Miriam's , laughter and song ever present in our rhythms. The poem in this collection called *Nara Swing* stands for the melody of poetics still so very alive in the Kalahari Desert.

Thanks you also Dr. Nelson Mandela for being so bighearted a person in standing up for your life and the future of so many South Africans. Moreover, for peoples in the world thirsting for the gifts of freedom, you, President Mandela, are a dazzling beacon. Embodied *In the Spirit of Nelson Mandela and his Comrades of Robben Island,* I have tried to encapsulate this love.

This ode to friendship and love goes out to all friends and families who've been an essential part of our life's journeys together.
I also would like to express appreciation for photographs and artistic impressions: Natisha, Philip T. , Peter & Marie-Claude, and Judith.

Thanks to the Great Spirit for life, love, and sustenance.

Contents

The Gift Of Freedom

In the Spirit of Nelson Mandela and his Comrades of Robben Island

Dreams Are Mirrors Of Light

On An Ice Cream Wave

Three Veiled Beauties from the Lakeshore

The Quiet Way Of Love

Frolic Unbridled

A Conversation Under Rainy Skies

Blucberry Mousse Cake-of-Life

Fast Winds Flash By Lac St. Louis

Nara Swing

Splattered Leaves of Autumn

Spring Yellow Willows

Roland Allen or "The Cat" - who was that Hot Sketch?

Keeping Faith

Dispelling Anger

Let Go Of Purloined Grapes

Dreamkeepers of the Fire For Freedom

Of Beaten Plastic and Twisted Heart

The Coptic Cross at St George's Cathedral Cape Town

Watercress Epilogue

The Gift Of Freedom

In the Spirit of Nelson Mandela and his Comrades of Robben Island

Dreams Are Mirrors Of Light

On An Ice Cream Wave

Three Veiled Beauties from the Lakeshore

Amandla! Power To The People!

In the Spirit of Nelson Mandela and his Comrades of Robben Island yellow and green dots of google mail?

On that crisp July morning of 1998 we crossed the lilting ocean
from Cape Town Waterfront for Robben Island's devotion.
The *Makana* powerboat virile and sure,
surged through thick silky waters great.
Mauve Table Mountain majesty made my chest inflate.
Foamy waters flashed under our feet like a path of slate.

Once we landed on this starkly grey green brown beautiful land,
we took the tour that was like parched earth so bland.
Then we encountered the limestone quarries that slammed
our still sleepy minds.
That's where Nelson Mandela
and his comrades used to hack out limestone rinds.

Our guide and former inmate pointed to an unmarked grave,
which hovered in our pensive minds.
A fellowman who'd given his life in service of honour-
trapped in a desolate hole in the ground in total horror!
Might his comrade next door
have been Mandela, Kathrada, or September?

This is what the burial mound helps us to remember.
In a six -by- four feet battleship doom,
you could very well feel the gloom.
Yet, I thought I "heard" the blank verse reverberate:
wait a minute. Why yes; was that a rhythm inchoate?
Dull sheen on a stainless washbasin showed signs of a former rinse.

For lack of resonating glint, my spleen did wince.
Prison-issue threadbare woollen blanket neatly folded, a whelp from me did evince.
It bespoke untold reams of stubborn monuments and Covenants made to a whiter god.
It justified this Alcatraz. The island;
the Count of Monte Cristo's and
Dante's Inferno- this insular quad.

Tarnished knife and fork lay limply
on the plate like a Daliesque surrealistic clock,
all trampled and bent out of shape-

with tempo, rhythm, and harmony; even though to the naked eye, alas, it appeared
to be functional.
Functional for only the tragic memories of a life charged electric with blood, prison
notes, and memories to fuel the flames of liberty for real.

Must've been a beggar's picnic that unveiled this obscene travesty of justice.
Rocky soggy moldy bread festered in hearts emboldened by pain.
Breaking stone for aeons is what the unrelenting boring hammer drilled into ever
rebellious souls.
Khaki-uniformed men and constant din
of rapping pick hammers drove them mad.

Cracking, splitting spitting, snarling tones, hacking coughs and curses
Could still puncture the early afternoon murmur issuing from the damp air.
Neatly folded threadbare blanket you did not comfort me aught.
Hard iron cell bars helped me naught.
I prayed as my eyes teared.

Nelson Mandela I thanked you for your person so revered.
We'll never forget that your bed was made of thorns too.
You gave the best years of your life true.
Yet, you came back like the lion of Africa to hone yourself so blue.
Rivonia ideals for a non-racial South Africa came to roost.

Bile in my mouth made me gulp and gave my heart a boost.
Awesome aura of your majestic presence still lingered in the light.
I felt pride rise up.
Some fears still prickled my earlobes,
as I heard the guide's rememberances through tortured robes.

My mind refused to budge
as my legs carried me sluggishly to the next stop of the hejiriac tour,
I looked down to see if my feet still touched the floor.
Then we edged to the next apparent station-of-the-cross.
For now it seemed clear that Mandela's cell is a still chapel.

A chapel, dedicated to freedom for
the peoples of our Mother Earth who hunger for the door;
the door to letting gilded wings fly free-
way high above the *bodhi* tree.
Bright blue sky slapped me awake from my reverie.

In the sterile stone courtyard of slavery,
as the stories of bondage unlocked,

my world shuddered.
A tumult arose in my soul.
Far far away in the Atlantic deep, I detected the seasick roll.

Waves drowned the executioner's song.
Arrested by the strong fresh breeze
I knew it would not be long
before the annals were told.
Stillness supreme did unfold.
Cold concrete benches became anchors.

Yes, chains tied down, rapidly flying,
cascading fractured old tiles layered on
the last stanchions of Apartheid-
finally denied with the promise of no more hate.
Playful gulls merry cries
rolled over splashing waves.

Sudden shudders raved and
welled up in my chest.
As a new day dawned bless'd
I cried inside and outside with wondrous release
in the knowledge that this scourge
signed forever its demise.

Unspoken words tumbled into my ears
made my being transformed by years.
Absolution caressed my wounds – excised from past gore.
Spent and tranquil went I ashore.
O Purple Mountain you spoke to me from the millennia.
You stood to witness forgiveness from dementia.

Dreams are Mirrors Of Light

Dreams are mirrors of light that resonate
in deepest wishes, fancies, ambitions, and plays.
Stature of goals, success, drives, power, money, and fame put a heavy weight on
the shape and size of our behaviours.
So let's start to build house anew
that's built on the rock of ages for endless times of hope.

Ocean-wide curtains of freedom
Heaploads of love,
bucketsful of joy,
forests of laughter
rivers of tears
seep into jugs of irony.

Mountainous visions-of eternity embrace
our common humanity.
Then let the mirrors shine.
Diamond galaxies of stars
reflect in your face, shining radiantly in your dreams
and in the mirrors of your heart.

From Khayelitsha and Crossroads to Muizenberg Beach, the future loomed supreme.
Cresting waves of gentle waves promised to bring a new dawn.

On An Ice Cream Wave

The morning is cool and fresh.
Gulls cry out joyously in
The early sun sitting in the Eastern sky.

Another train rumbles by on top of
Shuddering whitewashed trestles -
Tranquillity often broken by the ugly reminder.

Somehow the open shady beach
does not belong to me.
Just for today it will.

I munch through
a slice of buttered bread.
It feels like Christmas Day.
Dad has gotten a few days off for the Holidays.

We came to the beach with
Our picnic basket
filled with holiday goodness.
There is a low rumble- as crowds start to spillllll out of happy trains.

They rush to dip toes into cool water.
By noon we float on
ice cream waves,
We shine enthralled with our patch of paradise.

For all those people who love and make a better life for others.

The Quiet Way of Love

An unending fountain of mirth
The strength of a steel bar,
grace of a swan,
Never do you hear her utter defeat.

Yet deep down in blueberries
Encrusted in ivory sundae eyes,
looking out at the world,
breathes silver magic.

Gnarled, lacerated tired limbs
and smiles, laughs, grimaces abound.
You Never disapprove of
every breath of precious life.

Bestowed by life's tree that
gives the milk of youth, you
share laughter, whimsy, and mischief,
It is the quiet way of love.

Sunshine rises when
skies are ashen grey.
Rain patters on taut nerves-
snow rushes past my ears.

All of a sudden,
I see!
Everything comes together
through the portals of my soul.

Memories of warm Springs nights in Cape Town's neighbourhoods of Bo Kaap, District Six, Athlone of the 1950s and 1960s evoke mirage moments in Lachine, Quebec.

Three Veiled Beauties from the Lakeshore

As they walk to and from the water
They pass me and I gasp at their beauty.
Their dark shining eyes and flowing robes,
aromas of fine flowery perfumes
waft across the warm Spring air.
They sail along with chatter and light laughter.

Onward go they through the magical evening air.
I must turn around to watch them walk so close together
as they animatedly talk- delightfully of the sweet joys of womanhood.
Alas! the mystique sits behind the veil.
Forever a mere reflection hides within the trappings of the dress.
Through the keyhole of my heart they glide away.

Frolic Unbridled

A Conversation Under Rainy Skies

Blueberry Mousse Cake-of-Life

Fast Winds Flash By Lac St. Louis

Nara Swing

Splattered Leaves of Autumn

Spring Yellow Willows

Roland Allen or "The Cat" - who was that Hot Sketch?

South Africa forbade Black and White people from communication with each other up to Apartheid's abolition in South Africa's transition to a more democratic dispensation in 1994
'Tis a sin to even think of not letting people be and talk to each other for whatever reason, let alone for the colour of their skins. Rain go and cleanse murky souls and bring back the joy of human bonds not bondage.

A Conversation Under Rainy Skies

There is such a special fun
In talking under umbrellas cascaded by rainy skies.
Like a cool earthy corner of a garden
or by the water tank in a graveyard
where you can commune
with spirits that talk to you
of times past your horizons.

Brilliant soft petals
flash across your brow.
Knees hurt as you toil
at weeding the tea shower
which shrouds your ancestral home.
Mother touches on your head.

You speed across time
to fondest memories of
tears spent on life's
bittersweet droplets.
Narcissian-snow-spattered
on pinpricks of egg yolk.

Eyes, ears,
smell taste,
touch,
clear laughter
Shines with
golden lustre
through the water of life.

To catch the flight of an ostrich is so elusive a takeoff. When it seems that feathers will fly, staying earthbound is this bird's destiny.
I once rode an ostrich at Highgate Farms Oudtshoorn, South Africa
And Oh, what a ride it was!
And yet there is something there that reminds me of the thrill of relishing Blueberry Mousse-Cake-of Life as I contemplated the golden ostrich on the ruddy Fall Lachine evening sky.

Blueberry Mousse Cake-of-Life

Embrace more of life
as if it were a blueberry mousse cake,
in the milky azure sky,
atop which nests a golden frothy
white fillament of whipped whey-
soft and still in its supreme delight;
poised majestic- unmoved by gale or eddy.

Images from Le Grande Jetée
jump out at me with the
Sun setting
on blueberry mouse cake--
dimming gold,
burnished red,
russet gold and brown.

Three sister oaks stand erect
near 42nd Avenue on
the Lakeshore are almost bare,
except for a few spare dried leaves
at the very edges of time…
dry and ready to fall,
I almost caught a magical dropping leaf!

Young man caught
in the moment smiles.
Single gull danced before the setting sun
Topiary of wild maple leafs
came home on a golden path
bathed in pale blue sky;
reflected on gently swaying waters.

Red-tipped bushes made me see
that to dance with the sun at 5 o'clock
put me onto the back of a golden ostrich.
What was in the sky?
As gulls waltzed to the sunset serenade,
the Cosmos chimed to mystic keys.

I grew heady in my holy
joyous mesmerization.
Birds gamboled recklessly into the dawning twilight sky.

I stood rooted to the spot.
The sun branding its closing rays
upon my forehead straight to my heart.
What an eternity seemed to cruise by.

The shape of the golden ostrich
in the heavens above, of solid gold
struck the freedom chord
as church bells struck melodic chords at 5 o'clock
while gamboling through blueberry mousse cake.
Make this collage a homage
to embracing sweet life.

The winds of change need to blow anew across Africa's rugged face.

Fast Winds Flash By Lac St. Louis

Fall winds flash by Lac St. Louis—
splash dash,
torquing walking squeaking,
boat landing reeling.
Trees barely stay standing.
Suddenly a billy goat goes a' bleating.

Like underwater bagpipes ringing;
no sign single boats,
cold enough for a bowl of oats,
waves show no let up.
Docks groan loudly like rocking raves.
Who were those invisible knaves?

Gulls swoop in the frigid air
and switch into a quick run
into the blue sky and golden sun.
Green, gold, yellow, and brown
erases any grouche's frown.
Moods are instantly washed as all rust gets boshed.

Billowy are the sparse nimbus clouds.
Ducks delight in making their rounds.
Lac St. Louis your forward run
puts me in the mood for fun.
I love the voices crackling out stout.
I heard the wind just shout, *get all the children out!*

Get up!
Bring your warm cup.
Ready yourself for swift moves
into crisp rifts of your grooves
Did you say, 'what the...?
Or, did the blue heron utter, *sacré bleu?*

Can you imagine the fish from the Lake?
Especially if you had to sup on hake?
No, no nawwww!
I shall not eat hake raw.

Rather throw me in the icy water.
Please don't tell my daughter.

So follow the imp inside the windy screams
to discover your dreams.
Then find yourself laughing uproariously,
waxing ever so gloriously.
Fast winds you knock my breath away
as you careen swiftly away.

Enshrining fullness of Spirit in our lives and helping others to survive must certainly be our privilege. The victory dance of the San after the High Court decision to repatriate traditional lands so inspired Nara Dance and the ongoing thirst for spiritual and material sustenance. I dedicate this poem to the indigenous people of the world working to reclaim their heritages. In this crowd was a man who stood out and this is really his joyous ode to freedom.

Nara Swing

Take away the arid hurts of long desert eternities.
Let the night hold together tender friendships.
Nara feeds hot dry throats.
Time unseals long forgotten song.
Minds unfold.
I see vibrant azure mirage lie to me of clear spring water.
In my chest thunder beats incessantly.
I hear the call of my forefathers resonate with the Voice of the Universe.

Nativistic bells ring.
I leap high up in the air.
You prance like a prize pony.
I roll with the steadily pounding drum.
Spines shift towards the sun. I float, I sail, I shimmy, I circulate;
like wild wind you catapult backwards,
Brilliant red fire rages on.
Stick figures undulate in the blaze.

Trills of laughter race through deep glens of night's velvet promise.
Gibbous moon slowly rising raise specters
of hunger drawn tight with leather strops.
It's been six days and still no sign of food-
I bite into my lower lip.
Do you know what hunger feels like?
Delusions of elusive Nature's steer
haunt my hungry heart.

Hoarded wants can drive one barmy.
I try not to dwell on the pit in my stomach.
Breaking into the ravaging deep Unknown,
Num forges headlong into my throat into Kalaharian immortalities.
Warm wheels light up jittery legs
and now you saunter into miasmic trance
I'm grabbed easily into the fray;
the guardian of the dance beckons us

Horrible hysterical cries screech from afar.
I ease up;
you laugh deliriously with your head.
I float across the ever purple skyline
as blue green hues dart across your eyes,
cool mist fans my brow.

Body, mind, and soul travel as one in holy repose
Loving Mother Earth you root me firmly.

You made me rise above my stomach
to show me worlds I never thought I could go to before.
Now we dance carefreely into the freedom of the desert.
Sunshine disa light up my way tonight.
Sacred nara quench my parched memories.
Bring your bounty to my people.
Let them go where plenty is supreme;
anointed with your warm touch, O Great Spirit.

Shattered dreams are often the glass shards of along forgotten dismembered kaleidoscope. When shaken, pieces make dreams whole again.

Splattered Leaves of Autumn

Splattered leaves all soggy and matted,
All over the path green grass plaited.
Trees are half bare:
pale greens, bold browns, brassy reeds,
pink hoary bushes and weeds.
Warm winds flare up.

Choppy waters fill my cup.
Sole explorer meanders
to the end of the pier.
Two gulls gaily dance on
the wind against grey sky as palettes.
Leaping ballerinas afore shimmering silver barrettes.

Luminous curtain is being drawn
on the approaching end of Fall.
Girls and boys wear rainclothes
in damp soccer fields,
playing with wild abandonment
outside a private school.

A wiry girl plays the trombone
like she's glued to it like a limpet.
Raven-haired boy wields a bass clarinet.
Barely grasping the alto saxophone,
yet another boy plays the music of Stanley Clarke,
and it's almost turning dark.

They hear or see nothing but the jazz they belt out innocently.
I was an audience of one in the weather ghastly.
I cheer, I revel in their momentous joy.
Skylight streaks of yellow gold and black begin to spike
shadowy clouds alike.
Reluctantly I grasp my bike
And take a hike.

The Willow trees along the Liesbeeck River in Newlands, Cape Town South Africa remind me of the Lakeshore's grandeur.

Spring Yellow Willows

Spring makes me feel like a bride,
walking under a heady canopy,
like yellow umbrella spokes.
Canopy stretches across blue sky,
as you tread across a carpet of cushiony yellow beads and green grass.
Can you hear the misty rain gently falling through the roof?
Enveloped in warm slipcovers of fresh air,
grace and joy are wedded with Nature.
That was one heady foggy spring afternoon.
The air thick with promise of hotter days ahead.
Yeah! Summer will roll in soon.

Roland Allen or "The Cat" - who was that Hot Sketch?

The Cat was an exceptionally subtle teacher.
Really, could get under all students' skins or any creature.
His obvious zest for the things that lit his jolly eyes;
no, he did not care about the size of your parents' wallets or their lifestyles.
The colour of your skin, or the shape of your drawing;
or, whether you were a girl or a boy, The Cat stayed reassuring.

Through thick or thin, The Cat was in the relay.
Mainly, he loved life and to stay in play.
He worshipped the light fantastic.
He took an extraordinary interest in conveying this to all his students that he was a fanatic.
Roland's charisma would get to you too slowly; surely like the quiet fire of a smouldering volcano would reach you subtly.

Speak of someone who inspired me.
And also got to mates like John, Mervyn, and Noursie.
John reminded me that our late great Standard 6/ Grade 8 art teacher,
Mr. Roland Allen, in that Roland became known as The Jazz Cat or Katjie so dear.
His cool stealth;
his reverence for the late Rahsaan Roland Kirk's musical wealth.

Gregarious Hawaiian patterned tropical shirts with giant lapels,
avant garde everything,he sported, including Brylcreem gels;
Benny Stilborg from the Sea Point brought us the vibe,
as Roland stood head in hand enraptured in rhythmic tribe.
Breaking barriers of art, music, politics-
electrifying passions were Roland's ethics.

A permanent grimace
Seemed to hang around his edifice.
The corners of Roland's eyes and mouth
were both painted joyful and pained while going South.
Cougar eyes like grey stone,
 panther-like gait that betrayed that often he stood firm alone.

He held an unbridled kind of *joie de vivre*.
at dance, song, rhythm, or fever.
The pure joy of lithe movement and syncopations
that so typified feline grace, bespoke his motions.
 Roland was the real deal
For, up his sleeve he held the reel.

The Cat was an outstanding man long before he was deemed 'coloured'
by the apartheid government's synthetic maladies of race run rabid.
He was light skinned and had soft curly hair like a wire terrier.
He had left his soul behind in some Welsh village near here.
Enraptured in the bachannalian brilliance of Dylan Thomas,
he breathed such meaning into Under Milkwood f'r us.

Why, he should have been the original poster boy
for Ezra Keats poems on "Cats", ahoy!
He could appreciate any child's stick figure drawing
as portent with fun, mystery, meaning, and pure delight!
He defied all cardboard cutout definitions of "Art".
He lived and breathed the spirit of human life from the start.

Then its grotesque and beautiful depictions
of Art imitating life, he brought us to our sweet conclusions.
His lively twinkly eyes lit up sprightly
when he spoke of Dali or Dada's works of art daily.
A huge fan of Dali's eccentricisms besides,
we'd all split our sides.

Though, The Cat never sported a half *mustacchio*,
Roland's legendary shaving-cum-wine mug nary did see any *cappuccinio*,
Bottles of *Lieberstein* went with his fine canvasses,
soaked fine jazz collection often made for many sodden happy morasses,
thereby bringing a new dimension to the meaning of student and teacher
interactions.

Neill, Colin, Lew were all jazzmates
all grooved at scenes and sessions.
Just crazy about Coltrane,
Lateef, Ella, and
all the greats.
Roland writ large you burn bright in our grates.

Keeping Faith

Dispelling Anger

Let Go Of Purloined Grapes

Dreamkeepers of the Fire For Freedom

Of Beaten Plastic and Twisted Heart

The Coptic Cross at St George's Cathedral Cape Town

Watercress Epilogue

Peace will come to all who ask for it with real desire and sincerity of purpose-Chief Luthuli, President Nelson Mandela, President, Frederick W. de Klerk, Archbishop Desmond Tutu, Nobels for Peace.

Dispelling Anger

The anger I have opened
should now go to the seven winds.
There is no corner for it any longer
as I learn to find the words; the mood,
The tones to get beyond the wall of resentment.

It is the cool waters of the spirit that cleanse
the rushing current.
To love selflessly is becoming something
that I can do once more because of
a higher freedom to fly to
caverns that resound with organs of blue sweet melodies.

There are no shadows to deflect
the music of the dawn.
As the sun's rays
pierce ever so gently
into new crevices of my mind.

Let go of forbidden fruits and keep truth close by your side. For I dreamt I could fly to places high where birds have no race, prison, or chains.

Let Go Of Purloined Grapes

Touch not with faith
the purloined grapes filled with envy.
Wrap your whims around the flight
of Canada geeses' joyous flights gone happy-go-lucky.

Soaring through paths of wonderment, joy, and vast danger
so that when you reach the shore,
the ocean seems to swallow you up
in its velvety warm embrace of hope, storm, of shelter.

From the clangy siren that calls your name,
from the depths of the bottomless pit,
in which resides the endless din
of unfed souls, who cry for help.

Am I so blind to see
that I stand mired in mucky oozy soil?
Even though I see the distant golden
sun far away?

Yet there is a rope
that ties us all together
to the source of our fates
in the wildest lakes of human sighs.

Keep your eyes on the prize!

Dreamkeepers of the Fire For Freedom

To dream of freedom writ secure
is still the elusive key.
For no matter how far
or near the dream may be,
valiance must keep alive
the dreamkeepers of
the memory held high for
the fire, the light, the sound
of eternal drive
for fresh blooms of
glorious liberty every day!

The lust for gold in the depths of Gauteng turned men and women to plastic stilts.

Of Beaten Plastic and Twisted Heart

Can you feel the heartbeat
in the mangled distant din?
Do you hear the drone
of the false tone?

The slaves of misbegotten dreams
struggle and gag in giddy hoarse screams,
as the white dray beats the bag of moldy oats
that once resembled lively groats.

Do you dare to sing a note
through the choking in your throat?
As you break down in a pile,
in your stomach it feels vile.

Yet you try to brave a smile
in the winters of your wile.
Now go on and flay your guile
on the wheel of filthy file.

Where none can but revile
the coursing of the rim,
built on plastic
that makes the heart go mastic,
of beaten plastic and twisted heart
Run from there to a new start!

The Coptic Cross also called the Ethiopian Cross

The Coptic Church is the Christian church of Egypt, established by Mark in the 1st century (around 60 A.D.). The church now has dioceses elsewhere in Africa and the Near East. The early Gnostics and Copts adapted the Egyptian Ankh Cross as the basis of its emblem, which then evolved as the region's history changed.

Old Coptic crosses often incorporate a circle; sometimes large, sometimes small. The circle was inherited from the Ankh Cross, where it originally depicted the sun god. For the Coptic Church, the circle represents the eternal and everlasting love of God, as shown through Christ's crucifixion. It also symbolises Christ's halo and resurrection.

Whatever shape or form, the Coptic Cross usually has quite an elaborate design, reflecting the richness of the hearts of people in the Coptic church.

The Coptic Cross at St George's Cathedral Cape Town

Blessed barnacled black crust lacquered cross
What is the tale you bear in your shiny glass vault?
In silent witness stood I before your magnificence
Paying homage to your majesty just as earliest worshippers did in your native
Ethiopia, neither Eastern nor Western you remain anchored down in African soil.

Your luminescence spoke to me in unchaste tongues.
I feel as though I had known you for all of my born days.
For too long you'd been locked away from
prying eyes and now your virginity
was on display for the entire world to see.

My journey back to my homeland
after twenty four years abroad made your munificence even more special...
your quiet message spoke invoked binding sentiments
of One Continent in Mother Africa, within One World.
The booming resonance of your unstruck tones
reverberated from behind polished glass.

Ecumenical ties radiated from your core.
Your sandy crusty face echoed volumes of your wizened lore.
Speak no more

o dear Coptic Cross.
You touched my heart
o Coptic Cross of yore.

The end is merely a new beginning

Watercress Epilogue

Orange blossoms sweet organdy tablecloths flutter in the breeze.
Buttery puffs melt in the mouth.
Apricot jam from Swellendam sticks to my palate.
Hannepoot grapes from Constantia lighten my senses,

Tofu caramel cupcakes make me dizzy,
Savoury veggie meat pasties weigh heavily in my pack.
Hummus in olive canapés brush by my fingers;
orators bleating doggerel in the morning.

Can you hear the monstrous waves from Kalk Bay relentlessly smashing the dock?
Watercress from the *vlei* – is Mrs. Amon's well kept secret.
Dogeared photocopied lies lean against tarnished headstones in Woltemade
Cemetery.
Wolraad's bravery certainly must chase away the dirge of Apartheid.

Glossary

Hannepoot	A delicious juicy muscat grape variety grown in South Africa
Lieberstein	A white wine
Nara	(Acanthosicyos horridus) is a cucurbit plant endemic to the Namib desert. It is an important source of food and water for the San community along the rivers on the coastal side of Namibia.
Num	The life force, energy, or spirit.
Vlei	A Stream.

References

Coptic Cross
Copyright http://www.seiyaku.com/customs/crosses/coptic.html

FAO (2006). *Nara information.* Retrieved from
http://www.fao.org/DOCREP/003/X6694E/X6694E02.htm ma October 17.. [no underlining]

Seiyaku.com (2006). *Coptic Cross background* information. Rretrieved from
http://www.seiyaku.com/customs/crosses/coptic.html February 6.

Note

Wolraad Woltemade (c.1708 - June 1, 1773) was a South African dairy farmer, who died while rescuing sailors from the wreck of the ship De Jonge Thomas in Table Bay on 1 June 1773.

www.ingramcontent.com/pod-product-compliance
Lightning Source LLC
Chambersburg PA
CBHW080637290526
45790CB00007B/3100